THE ALI ABBASI
JOKE BOOK

D0532402

Proceeds from the sale of this book
will go to the Kenny Macintyre Sports
Park Memorial Trust in order
to refurbish the existing football
ground in Tobermory, Isle of Mull.

THE ALI ABBASI
JOKE BOOK

Ali Abbasi

Foreword by Fred MacAulay

The Vital Spark

The Vital Spark is an imprint of
Neil Wilson Publishing
303a The Pentagon Centre
36 Washington Street
GLASGOW
G3 8AZ
Tel: 0141-221-1117
Fax: 0141-221-5363
E-mail: nwp@sol.co.uk
http://www.vitalspark.co.uk/

A catalogue record for this book is available
from the British Library.

ISBN 1-903238-03-X
Typeset in Ellington
Designed by Mark Blackadder

Printed by WS Bookwell

Acknowledgements

In the course of compiling this wee book, I've received help from a number of sources, many of whom prefer to remain anonymous! Some are not so bashful though, and I am grateful to Glasgow taxi driver Jim Reid, Cameron Clark, Paula Smith, Roshan Abbasi, Alan McPhee, Alison Di Rollo, the late Tommy Cooper, Colin Mackinnon, John Beattie, Jack McConnell and Stewart Prodger, owner of www.mirth.co.uk, and everyone else who helped and whose names I have just plain forgotten.

Also my grateful thanks to Fred MacAulay for taking the time to pen the foreword.

Contents

Foreword by Fred MacAulay

As regular listeners to my radio show ... (92-95 FM) ... (810 medium wave) ... (8.45 till 10) ... (Radio Scotland) ... will know, Ali Abbasi is never short of a joke to start the hour off after the 9am news and travel. Whilst the origin and political correctness are often dubious (that's the joke, not Ali) any joke is delivered in his own inimitable style with typical Ali aplomb. I take my hat off to him for the effort he has put into compiling this book and I look forward to seeing the fruits of his labours in the football ground in Tobermory. It'll be a fitting testament to the friendship Ali shared with his late pal Kenny.

I'd advise a map of the West Coast of Scotland for any foreign nationals who have bought this book, in order that you may fully enjoy the Tiree minister gag on page 61. My personal favourite is the octopus joke on page 54.

Along with 'Where's Ally?' and 'What does Aggie Elsden look like?' the most frequently asked question I hear is 'What was Ali Abbasi's *ugly woman in the supermarket* gag?' Well it looks like Ali has decided that this should remain a mystery. Or maybe it'll be the first joke in book two ... I know he's determined to see that football ground refurbished! Enjoy.

Fred MacAulay

Welcome to Glasgow ...and football!

A MAN was walking down Byres Road when he noticed a most unusual funeral procession on its way to the Necropolis. A long black hearse was followed by a second long black hearse about 50 feet behind. Behind the second hearse was a solitary man walking a pit bull terrier on a lead. Behind him were 200 men walking single file. The man couldn't stand the curiosity. He respectfully approached the man walking the dog and said 'Sir, I know now is a bad time to disturb you, but I've never seen a funeral like this. Whose funeral is it?' The man replied 'Well, that first hearse is for my wife.'

'What happened to her?' The man replied 'My dog attacked and killed her.'

He inquired further, 'Well, who is in the second hearse?'

The man answered, 'My mother-in-law. She was trying to help my wife when the dog turned on her.'

A poignant and thoughtful moment of silence passes between the two men. 'Sir, could I borrow that dog?'

'Get in line.'

ONE FOGGY day in October, a man is killing some time by walking in an area of the City of London that he has never been through before. Down a dimly lit alleyway he notices a curious little shop selling antiques. After a moment's reflection he walks into the shop, and starts examining the many weird and wonderful items. Looking around, he notices a life-sized bronze sculpture of a cat in a dark corner. The sculpture is so intriguing, he decides he must buy it and asks the shopkeeper the price. 'Twelve pounds for the cat, Sir,' the shopkeeper tells him, 'and 100 pounds for the story that goes with it.' 'I'll take the cat,' says the man, 'but you can keep the story.' The transaction completed, the man leaves the store with the bronze cat under his arm.

As he crosses the street in front of the store, two cats emerge from an alley and fall into step behind him. Nervously looking over his shoulder, he begins to walk faster, but every time he passes another alley, more cats come out and follow him. By the time he's walked two streets, at least a hundred cats are at his heels, and people are beginning to point and shout. He walks even faster, and soon breaks into a trot as multitudes of cats swarm from valleys, basements, and abandoned cars.

Thousands of cats are now at his heels, and as he sees the river at the bottom of the hill, he panics and starts to run full pelt. No matter how fast he runs, the cats keep up, hissing insanely, now in their thousands. He looks up and sees that he is approaching the River Thames, and the trail of cats is now several hundred yards long behind him. Making a mighty leap, he jumps onto a lamp post, grasping it with one arm while he hurls the bronze cat into the river with the other. Clinging to the lamp post, he watches in amazement as the seething tide of cats surges past him into the river, where they all drown.

Amazed and dumbfounded, he makes his way back to the antique shop. 'Ah, so you've come back for the story,' says the shopkeeper. 'No,' says the man, 'I was wondering if you have a bronze Rangers' fan?'

A MAN bumps into a pal and sees that his car is a total write-off, covered with leaves, grass, branches, dirt and blood. He asks his friend, 'What's happened to your car?'

'Well,' the friend replies, 'I ran over Mark Viduka'

'OK,' says the man, 'that explains the blood. But what about the leaves, the grass, the branches and the dirt?'

'Well, he tried to escape through the park.'

FOR THE football fans amongst you, a few of the squads have just been announced for the 2002 World Cup:

BRAZIL

Pinnochio Libero Vimto Memento
Borneo Tango
Stereo (L) Cheerio Subbuteo Stereo (R)
Portfolio

SUBS:
Placebo
Porno
Aristotle

DENMARK

Toomanigoalssen Tryandstopussen Crapdefenssen Haveagossen
Firstsson Secondsson
Thirdsson Legshurtssen Notroubleseeingussen Wherestheballssen
Getthebeerssen

SUBS:
Howmanygoalsisthatssen
Finallygaveupcountinssen
Hurryupandblowthewhistlessen
Palofalexfergussen

ITALY

Baloni Potbelli Beerbelli Giveitsumwelli
Wotsontelli Toonsgotkenni
Onetoomani Legslikejelli Havabenni Wobblijelli
Spendapenni

SUB:
Cantthinkofani

Just before the Wembley play-off for the Euro 2000 championship, there is a lightning strike which kills Kevin Keegan and Craig Brown. They ascend into heaven and are met at the pearly gates by the Boss himself.

'Welcome Gentlemen,' says God. 'Come on in, and I'll show you your accomodation.'

He takes Kevin by the hand and takes him for a short walk through fields of beautiful flowers until they come across a pretty cottage by a stream, with lovely flower beds and tall trees gently swaying in the breeze. The thatched roof forms the shape of a St George's cross.

'Gosh, Lord,' says Kevin, 'I don't know what to say.' God smiles at him, and taking Craig Brown by the hand, starts to walk back up the path. As they are walking away, Kevin looks around him, and a little further up the road he sees a gigantic Scots baronial castle topped with the Saltire flag and surrounded by fields of heather and stands of Scot's Pine and Douglas Fir.

A bit concerned, Kevin runs after God and Craig Brown and says: 'Excuse me, God, I'm deeply honoured and touched by the status of my wonderful new accomodation, and I don't wish to sound ungrateful or anything, but I was wondering why Graig's house is ... well, you know, so much bigger, and even grander than mine.'

God laughs, puts a consoling arm around Kevin's shoulder, and says to him softly, ' There, there, Kevin. That's not Craig's house ... it's mine!'

Ethnic, Cultural (and Irish)

THREE CONTESTANTS are on *Mastermind*: a Catholic, a Protestant and a Pakistani.

The question master asks the Protestant his chosen subject and he replies, 'The Reformation and John Knox from 1536 to 1572.'

The Catholic replies when asked, 'The Catholic Church from 1299 to 1499.'

When the Pakistani is asked he replies, 'ANORAKS from £10.99 to £15.99!'

GHANDI WALKED barefoot everywhere, to the point that his feet became quite thick and hard. Even when not engaging in a protest hunger strike, he ate little and became quite thin and frail. He was also a devoutly spiritual person, and, due to his irregular diet he developed extremely bad breath. As a result of all this, he forever became known as a:

Super-calloused fragile mystic plagued with halitosis.

AN ORIENTAL Asian man walks into a currency exchange bureau in Glasgow with 2000 rupees and walks out with £72. The next week he walks in with 2000 rupees, and gets £66. He asks the lady why he got less money this week than the previous week and the lady says 'Fluctuations'.

The man storms out, and just before slamming the door turns around and says, 'Fluc you clazy Scots too!'

LEARN CHINESE IN FIVE MINUTES

English phrase	**Chinese Interpretation**
Are you harbouring a fugitive?	Hu Yu Hai Ding?
See me ASAP	Kum Hia Nao
Stupid Man	Dum Gai
Small Horse	Tai Ni Po Ni
Your price is too high!!	No Bai Dam Ting!!
Did you go to the beach?	Wai Yu So Tan?
I bumped into a coffee table.	Ai Bang Mai Ni
I think you need a facelift.	Chin Tu Fat
It's very dark in here.	Wai So Dim?
Has your flight been delayed?	Hao Long Wei Ting?
That was an unauthorised execution.	Lin Ching
I thought you were on a diet.	Wai Yu Mun Ching?
This is a tow away zone.	No Pah King
Do you know the lyrics to the Macarena?	Wai Yu Sing Dum Song?
You are not very bright.	Yu So Dum
I got this for free.	Ai No Pei
I am not guilty.	Wai Hang Mi?
Please, stay a while longer.	Wai Go Nao?
Our meeting was scheduled for next week.	Wai Yu Kum Nao?
They have arrived.	Hia Dei Kum
Stay out of sight.	Lei Lo

He's cleaning his automobile.
Your body odour is offensive.

Wa Shing Ka
Hu Man Go!

CONFUCIUS SAY

Passionate kiss like spider's web, soon lead to undoing of fly.
Virginity like bubble, one prick all gone.
Man who run in front of car get tired.
Man who run behind car get exhausted.
Man who walk through airport turnstile sideways going to Bangkok.
Man with one chopstick go hungry.
Man who eat many prunes get good run for money.
Baseball is wrong, man with four balls cannot walk.
War doesn't determine who is right, war determines who is left.
Wife who put husband in doghouse soon find him in cathouse.
Man who fight with wife all day get no piece at night.
Man who drive like hell bound to get there.
Man who stand on toilet is high on pot.
Man who lives in glass house should change clothes in basement.
Man who farts in church sits in own pew.
Man who drops watch in toilet bound to have crappy time.

I MET a Chinese man who told me his name was Abe Schwartz. I asked him if he was Jewish, to which he replied that he wasn't. 'How did you get that name? Did your mother marry a Jewish man?'

'No, no. What happened was, when I came to this country and was standing on the immigration line, the man in front of me was named Abe Schwartz. When it came to my turn, they asked me my name and I said, "Sem Ting".'

TWO ITALIAN men get on a bus and take a seat behind a middle-aged lady. An animated conversation takes place between the two Italians. 'Emma come first. Den I come. Den two asses, dey come together. Den I come again. Two asses, dey come together again. I come again and pee twice. Den I come once more.' The lady looked around and angrily said, 'You filthy, foul mouthed swine! In this country, we don't talk about our sex lives in public!'

'You coola down, lady,' said the Italian. 'I'm-a just-a tellin my friend how to spell-a Mississippi'

What do you call an Indian karaoke singer?
Gupty Singh

What do you call an Indian swimming pool attendant?
Handyer Banden

AN OLD Native American chief was famous for predicting what the weather would do. A group of people went up to the chief and asked him, 'What will the weather be like tomorrow?' The chief replied, 'Much rain. Very wet.' The next day, it did rain and it was very wet. Some more people went up to the chief and asked, 'What will the weather be like tomorrow?' 'Much snow. Very cold.' Sure enough, it snowed and it was very cold. The next day, people were so impressed with this, they asked him again. Chief,' they asked, 'what will the weather do tomorrow?'

The chief replied, 'Me not know … transistor radio broken.'

RUNNING FOX was the bravest warrior in the Sioux tribe, and as such he was allowed three squaws. One night Running Fox was feeling a little frisky, so he crawled into the tepee of squaw number one. 'No!' she said, 'You cannot have your wicked way with me on the rough ground inside this tepee. If you want to make love you must make me a comfortable new blanket, from the hide of a buffalo!' Well, to a warrior of Running Fox's stature this was not a difficult request. He ran from the camp, quickly tracked a herd of buffalo, shot one with a bow and arrow, skinned it and made a lovely comfortable blanket. He took it back to squaw number one, who was delighted and they made love.

The next night Running Fox was again feeling a little frisky, so he crawled into the tepee of squaw number two. 'No!' she said, 'You cannot have your wicked way with me on the rough ground inside this tepee. If you want to make love you must make me a comfortable new blanket, from the hide of a mountain lion!' This was a little more tricky for Running Fox. He set off into the hills and hunted down a young mountain lion, cut its throat, skinned it and made a lovely comfortable blanket. He took it back to squaw number two, who was delighted with it and they then made love.

The next night Running Fox was again feeling a little frisky, so he crawled into the tepee of squaw number three. 'No!' she said, 'You cannot have your wicked way with me on the rough ground inside this teepee. If you want to make love you must make me a comfortable new blanket, from the hide of a hippopotamus!' Now, this was much more difficult, but Running Fox was never one to shy away from a challenge. He travelled to Africa, swam up the Zambezi River, found a hippopotamus, wrestled it with his bare hands, skinned it and made a lovely comfortable blanket. He took it back to squaw number three, who was delighted with it and so they made love.

It so happened that all three squaws became pregnant as a result of all this love-making. In due course squaw number one gave birth to a baby girl. The next day squaw number two gave birth to a baby boy. Finally, squaw number three gave birth to twins – one girl and one boy. Being a superstitious chap, Running Fox was sure there had to be some meaning behind this and so he consulted the tribe's wise man. 'Why,' Running Fox asked, 'did the squaw I made love to on a blanket made from buffalo hide have a baby girl, the squaw I made love to on a blanket made from mountain lion hide have a baby boy, and the squaw I made love to on a blanket made from hippopotamus hide have twins?'

The wise man looked up and said, 'It's all down to geometry!'

'What?' asked Running Fox.

The wise man continued, 'Pythagoras' theorem states that, "the squaw on the hippopotamus is always equal to the sum of the squaws on the other two hides!" '

A YOUNG man is wandering, lost, in a forest when he comes upon a small house. Knocking on the door he is greeted by an ancient Chinese man with a long beard. 'I'm lost,' said the young man. 'Can you put me up for the night?'

'Certainly,' the Chinese man said, 'but on one condition. If you so much as lay a finger on my daughter, I will inflict upon you the three worst Chinese tortures known to man.' 'OK,' said the man, thinking that the daughter must be pretty old as well, and entered the house.

Over dinner, the daughter came down the stairs. She was young, beautiful and had a fantastic figure. She was obviously attracted to the young man, since she couldn't keep her eyes off him during the meal. Remembering the old man's warning, he ignored her and went up to bed alone. During the night he could bear it no longer and sneaked into her room for a night of passion. He was careful to keep everything quiet so the old man wouldn't hear and, near dawn, he crept back to his room, exhausted but happy. He woke to feel a pressure on his chest. Opening his eyes, he saw a large rock on his chest with a note on it that read:

Chinese torture #1: Large rock on chest. 'Well, that's pretty lousy torture,' he thought. 'If that's the best the old man can do then I don't have much to worry about.' He picked the large rock up, walked over to the window and threw it out. As he did so, he noticed another note on it that read:

Chinese torture #2: Rock tied to left testicle. Panicking, he glanced down and saw that the rope was getting close to taut. Figuring that a few broken bones was better than castration, he jumped out of the window after the boulder. As he plummeted towards the ground, he saw a large sign on the ground that read:

Chinese torture #3: Right testicle tied to bedpost.

A JAPANESE man went to America for sightseeing. On the last day, he hailed a cab and told the driver to drive to the airport. During the journey, a Honda drove past the taxi. Thereupon, the man leaned out of the window excitedly and yelled, 'Honda, very fast! Made in Japan!'

After a while, a Toyota sped past the taxi. Again, the Japanese man leaned out of the window and yelled, 'Toyota, very fast! Made in Japan!' And then a Mitsubishi sped past the taxi. For the third time, the Japanese leaned out of the window and yelled, 'Mitsubishi, very fast! Made in Japan!'

The driver was a little angry, but he kept quiet. The antics went on for quite a number of cars. Finally, the taxi arrived at the airport. The fare was $300. The Japanese exclaimed, 'Wah … so expensive!'

The driver yelled back, 'Meter, very fast! Made in Japan!'

WHY ARE more black soldiers killed in wars than white soldiers ?
Because every time the captain shouts 'GET DOWN!' the black soldiers all get up and start dancing.

THE BEST CURRY SONGS EVER

Popadum Preach	Madonna
Korma Chameleon	Culture Club
Dansak Queen	Abba
You Can't Curry Love	Diana Ross and the Supremes
Tears On My Pilau	Kylie Minogue
It's Bhuna Hard Days Night	The Beatles
Girlfriend in a Korma	The Smiths
Pilau Talk	Doris Day
Vindaloo	Abba
Rice Rice Baby	Vanilla Ice
Love me Tandoor	Elvis Presley
We Don't Have to Tikka Clothes Off	Germaine Jackson
Bye Bye Balti	Bay City Rollers
Livin' Dhal	Cliff Richard
Raita Here, Raita Now	Fatboy Slim

How do you confuse an Irishman?
Put three shovels in front of him and ask him to take his pick.

Why wasn't Christ born in Ireland?
They couldn't find three wise men and a virgin.

Why don't they have ice in Ireland?
They lost the recipe.

AN IRISHMAN gets a job driving a one-man operated bus. Ten seconds after leaving the garage there's an almighty crash. The Depot Manager runs out and says to him 'Mick, what happened?' 'I don't know,' says Mick, 'I was upstairs collecting the fares at the time.'

BLOKE WALKS into an Irish fish and chip shop and says to Pat, the Irish owner 'Fish and chips twice, please.'
   'I heard you the first time,' says Pat.

TWO IRISHMEN on a building site – Paddy is eating a huge steak and kidney pie. Mick says to him, 'How heavy is that pie?' and Paddy says 'I don't know.' Mick says, 'Why don't you get it weighed?' 'Where could I do that?' asks Paddy. 'Over the rainbow,' says Mick. 'I don't understand,' says Paddy.
   'It's all in that song from *The Wizard of Oz*,' says Mick.
   'Somewhere over the rainbow, weigh a pie.'

TWO IRISHMEN are adrift on an iceberg.
Suddenly Mick shouts 'We're saved!'
Pat says 'How do you know that?'
Mick says 'Here comes the *Titanic*.'

Did you hear about the Irishman who drowned digging a grave for a friend who had died? He'd always wanted to be buried at sea.

TWO IRISHMEN are walking in a wood when they see a sign saying 'Tree Fellers Wanted'.
'Just our luck,' says Seamus, 'there are only two of us.'

MICK GOES to a building site to see if there are any jobs. The gaffer says 'I can't start you today but if you come tomorrow I might be able to give you a job cos I've got a feller here today who hasn't turned up. If he doesn't come tomorrow I'll send him home and you can have his job.'

DID YOU hear about the Irishman who went to the doctor and was given two weeks to live?
He asked for the last week in June and the first week in July.

Did you hear about the Irish jellyfish?
It set.

PADDY MISSED the local soccer match. When he met Mick later he asked the score.
'Nil-nil,' said Mick. 'What was it at half time?' said Paddy.
'I don't know,' said Mick, 'I was only there for the second half.'

PADDY AND Murphy were out fishing when the boat sprang a leak. Paddy said, 'It's alright, I've made another hole over there to let the water out.'

PADDY WENT to a Pizza Hut and ordered a large pizza. When it came, the waiter asked if he wanted it cut into four or six slices. 'Better make it four,' said Paddy 'I don't think I could eat six'.

Did you hear about the Irish Godfather?
He kept making people an offer he couldn't remember.

PADDY WAS digging a hole when Mick turned up. 'What are you doing?' asked Mick. 'Digging a hole to bury my dog,' said Paddy. 'What are the other three holes for?' said Mick. 'They were for the dog as well but they weren't big enough,' said Paddy.

Politics

A quick and easy-to-understand guide to political ideologies:

FEUDALISM
You have two cows. Your lord takes some of the milk.

FASCISM
You have two cows. The government takes both, hires you to take care of them, and sells you the milk.

PURE COMMUNISM
You have two cows. Your neighbours help you take care of them, and you all share the milk.

APPLIED COMMUNISM
You have two cows. You have to take care of them, but the government takes all the milk.

DICTATORSHIP
You have two cows. The government takes both and shoots you.

NIGERIAN DEMOCRACY
You have two cows. The government takes both, shoots you and sends the cows to Zurich.

MILITARISM
You have two cows. The government takes both and drafts you.

SINGAPOREAN DEMOCRACY
You have two cows. The government fines you for keeping two unlicensed farm animals in an apartment.

PURE DEMOCRACY
You have two cows. Your neighbours decide who gets the milk.

REPRESENTATIVE DEMOCRACY
You have two cows. Your neighbours pick someone to tell you who gets the milk.

AMERICAN DEMOCRACY
The government promises to give you two cows if you vote for it. After the election, the president is impeached for speculating in cow futures. The press dubs the affair 'Cowgate'. The cow sues you for breach of contract.

BRITISH DEMOCRACY
You have two cows. You feed them sheeps' brains and they go mad. The government doesn't do anything.

EUROPEAN DEMOCRACY
You have two cows. At first the government regulates what you can feed them and when you can milk them. Then it pays you not to milk them. After that it takes both, shoots one, milks the other and pours the milk down the drain. Then it requires you to fill out forms accounting for the missing cows.

CAPITALISM
You have two cows. You sell one and buy a bull.

HONG KONG CAPITALISM

You have two cows. You sell three of them to your publicly-listed company, using letters of credit opened by your brother-in-law at the bank, then execute a debt/equity swap with associated general offer so that you get all four cows back, with a tax deduction for keeping five cows. The milk rights of six cows are transferred via a Panamanian intermediary to a Cayman Islands company secretly owned by the majority shareholder, who sells the right to all seven cows' milk back to the listed company. The annual report states that the company owns eight cows, with an option on one more. Meanwhile, you kill the two cows because of bad Feng Shui.

LESBIANISM

You have two cows. They get married and adopt a veal calf.

TOTALITARIANISM

You have two cows. The government takes them and denies they ever existed. Milk is banned.

SURREALISM

You have two giraffes. The government requires you to take harmonica lessons

WHAT IS POLITICS?

A little boy goes to his dad and asks, 'What's politics?' Dad says, 'Well, son, let me try to explain it to you this way. I'm the breadwinner of the family, so let's call me "Capitalism". Your mum is the administrator of the household, so we'll call her "The Government". We're here to take care of YOUR needs so we'll call you "The People". The nanny works hard all day for very little money so we'll consider her "The Working Class". And your baby brother ...

we'll call him "The Future". Now, think about that and see if it makes sense.'

So, the little boy goes off to bed, thinking about what his dad has said. Later that night he hears his baby brother crying so he gets up to check on him. He finds that the baby has soiled his nappy, so the little boy goes to his parents' room and finds his mother sound asleep. Not wanting to wake her, he goes to the nanny's room. Finding the door locked, he peeks into the keyhole and sees his father in bed with the nanny. He gives up and goes back to bed.

The next morning, the little boy says to his father, 'Dad, I think I understand the concept of politics now.' The father says, 'Good, son, tell me in your own words what you think politics is about.'

The little boy replies, 'Well, while Capitalism is screwing the Working Class, the Government is sound asleep, the People are being ignored and the Future is in deep shit.'

TONY BLAIR is being shown around a hospital. Towards the end of his visit, he is shown into a ward with a number of people with no obvious signs of injury. He goes to greet the first patient and the chap replies:

'Fair fa' your honest sonsie face,
Great chieftain o' the puddin' race!
Aboon them a' ye tak your place,
Painch, tripe, or thairm:
Weel are ye wordy o' a grace
As lang 's my arm.'

Tony, being somewhat confused, grins inanely and moves on to the next patient and greets him. He replies:

'Some hae meat, and canna eat,
And some wad eat that want it,
But we hae meat and we can eat,
And sae the Lord be thankit.'

Tony turns to the doctor accompanying him and says, 'What sort of ward is this? A mental ward?'

'No,' replies the doctor, 'It's the Burns unit.'

A BUS load of politicians were driving down a country road when, all of a sudden, the bus ran off the road and crashed into a tree in an old farmer's field. The old farmer, after seeing what had happened, went over to investigate. He then proceeded to dig a hole to bury the politicians. A few days later the local sheriff came out, saw the crashed bus, and asked the old farmer where all the politicians had gone. The old farmer said he had buried them. The sheriff asked the old farmer, 'Were they all dead?' The old farmer replied, 'Well, some of them said they weren't, but you know how them politicians lie.'

BOB HOPE always admired politicians who prayed.

'They have their hands somewhere where you can see them.'

Police

Police arrested two kids yesterday, one was drinking battery acid, the other was eating fireworks.

They charged one and let the other one off.

Did you hear about the guy who broke into the razor blade factory?
He got nicked!

Did you hear about the guy who broke into a futon shop?
He didn't get caught but now he's laying low!

Did you hear about the guy who broke into the sex shop?
He got banged up!

Did you hear about the farmer who stole the horses' feed?
He got bale!

Did you hear about the guy who broke into the sandwich shop?
He got done for breach of the piece!

Did you hear about the guys who nicked the calendar?
They got six months each.

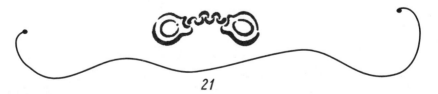

THERE WAS an old country sheriff who always said, 'It could have been worse.' No matter what happened, the old sheriff always had the same answer … 'It could have been worse.'

One day, two deputies in the sheriff's office answered an emergency call at a farmhouse. When they walked in, they found the nude bodies of a man and a woman in the bedroom. They had been shot to death. When they went to the living room, they found the body of a man with a gun at his side. 'No doubt about it,' one deputy said to the other. 'This was a double murder and suicide. This guy came home and found his wife in bed with somebody else and shot them both. Then he shot himself.' 'You're right,' the other deputy replied. 'Double murder and suicide. But I'll bet you when the sheriff gets here he's going to say … "It could have been worse." '

'No way. How could it have been worse? There are three people in the house, and all of them have been shot to death. It couldn't be worse. You're on.'

About that time, the old sheriff arrived at the scene. He walked into the bedroom and saw the two nude bodies. He then walked into the living room and saw the man on the floor with the gun by his side. 'No doubt about it,' the sheriff said, shaking his head. 'It was a double murder and suicide. This guy came home and found his wife in bed with somebody else and shot them both. Then he shot himself.' After hesitating for a moment, the old sheriff looked his deputies squarely in the eyes. 'But, you know,' he said, 'it could have been worse.' The deputy who had lost the bet jumped up and shouted, 'Sheriff, how could it have been worse? There are three people in this farmhouse, and all three of them are dead. It couldn't have been worse!'

'Yes it could,' the sheriff retorted. 'You see that guy there on the floor? If he had come home yesterday, that would be me there in that bed.'

THE POLICE arrived and found a woman dead on her living room floor with a golf club next to her body. They asked the husband, 'Is this your wife?'

'Yes,' he replied.

'Did you kill her?'

'Yes,' he replied.

'It looks like you struck her about eight times with this 3-iron. Is that correct?'

'Yes,' he replied, ' ... but could you put me down for a five?'

A POLICEMAN was terribly overweight and was getting heat from his sergeant and scathing remarks from his fellow officers. He was ordered to go on a diet. The department doctor put him on a special diet.

'I want you to eat regularly for two days, then skip a day, and repeat this procedure for two weeks. The next time I see you, you'll have lost at least five pounds.'

When the officer returned, he shocked the doctor by losing nearly 20 pounds. 'Why, that's amazing!' the doctor said, 'Did you follow my instructions?'

The officer nodded. 'I'll tell you though, I thought I was going to drop dead that third day.'

'From hunger, you mean?'

'No, from skipping.'

KELVIN COMES up to the Mexican border on his bicycle. He's got two large bags over his shoulders. The US border patrol officer stops him and says, 'What's in the bags?' 'Sand,' answered Kelvin. The officer says, 'We'll just see about that. Get off the bike.' The agent takes the bags and rips them apart; empties them out and finds nothing in them but sand. He detains Kelvin overnight and has the sand analysed, only to discover that there *is* nothing but pure sand in the bags. The officer releases Kelvin, puts the sand into new bags, hefts them onto the man's shoulders, and lets him cross the border.

A week later, the same thing happens. The officer asks, 'What have you got?' 'Sand,' says Kelvin. The officer does his thorough examination and discovers that the bags contain nothing but sand. He gives the sand back to Kelvin, and Kelvin crosses the border on his bicycle. This sequence of events is repeated every day for three years. Finally, Kelvin doesn't show up one day and the officer meets him in a cantina in Mexico. 'Hey, Buddy,' says the border patrol officer, 'I know you are smuggling something. It's driving me crazy. It's all I think about ... I can't sleep. Just between you and me, what is it that you're smuggling?' Kelvin sips his beer and says, 'Bicycles.'

PC BOB receives a free ticket to the Cup Final from his department for outstanding police work. Unfortunately, when Bob arrives at Wembley he realises the seat is in the last row in the corner of the stadium. About halfway through the first half, Bob notices an empty seat 10 rows back from the centre line, and he decides to take a chance and makes his way through the stadium and around the security guards to the empty seat. As he sits down, he asks the gentleman sitting next to him, 'Excuse me, is anyone sitting here?' The man says 'No.'

Very excited to be in such a great seat for the game, Bob again inquires of the man next to him, 'This is incredible! Who in their right mind would have a seat like this for the Cup Final and not use it?' The man replies, 'Well, actually, the seat belongs to me, I was supposed to come with my wife, but she passed away. This is the first

Cup Final we haven't been together at since we got married in 1967.'

'Well, that's really sad,' says Bob, 'but still, couldn't you find someone to take the seat? A relative or close friend?'

'No,' the man replies, 'they're all at her funeral.'

A DRUNKEN wino was stumbling down the street with one foot on the curb and one foot in the gutter. A copper pulls up and says, 'I've got to take you in, sir. You're obviously drunk.'

The wasted wino asks, 'Ociffer, are ya absolutely sure ah'm drunk?'

'Yeah, I'm sure,' says the copper. 'Let's go.'

Obviously relieved, the wino says, 'That's good then – I thought I was a cripple.'

LATE ONE Friday night a policeman spotted a man driving very erratically through the streets of Dublin. The officer pulled him over and asked him if he has been drinking that evening. 'Aye, so I have. 'Tis Friday, you know, and the lads stopped by the pub where I had six or seven pints. And then there was something called 'Happy Hour' and they served these mar-gar-itas which are quite good. I had four or five o' those. Then I had to drive me friend Mike home and o' course I had to go in for a couple of Guinness – couldn't be rude, ye know. Then I stopped on the way home to get another bottle for later.'

The man fumbled around in his coat until he located his bottle of whiskey, which he held up for inspection. The officer sighed, and said, 'Sir, I'm afraid I'll need you to step out of the car and take a breathalyser test.'

Indignantly, the man said, 'Why? Don't ye believe me?'

A PRIEST went into a Washington DC barbershop and got his hair cut. He then asked how much he owed the barber. 'No charge, Father,' the barber said. 'I consider it a service to the Lord.' When the barber arrived at his shop the next morning, he found a dozen small prayer booklets on the step along with a thank you note from the priest.

A few days later, a police officer came in. 'How much do I owe you?' the cop asked after his haircut. 'No charge, officer,' the barber answered. 'I consider it a service to my community.' The next morning the barber found a dozen doughnuts on the step along with a thank you note from the police officer.

A few days after that, a Senator walked in for a haircut. 'How much do I owe you?' he asked afterward. 'No charge,' the barber replied. 'I consider it a service to my country.' The next morning when he arrived at the shop, the barber found a dozen Senators waiting on the step.

AN AMISH lady is trotting down the road in her horse and buggy when she is pulled over by a cop. He says, 'Ma'am, I'm not going to ticket you, but I do have to issue you with a warning. You have a broken reflector on your buggy.'

'Oh, I'll let my husband, Jacob, know as soon as I get home.'

'That's fine,' the cop said. 'Another thing, ma'am. I don't like the way that one rein loops across the horse's back and around one of his balls. I consider that animal abuse. That's cruelty to animals. Have your husband take care of that right away.'

Later that day, she was telling her husband about her encounter with the cop. 'He said the reflector is broken,' the wife says.

'I can fix that in two minutes,' Jacob said. 'Anything else wrong?'

'I'm not sure, Jacob ... something about the emergency brake ... '

ONE COLD, but sunny winter morning, Bill Clinton is out jogging in the park. He is running past a big pile of snow, when he notices something strange. In the snow, 'BILL CLINTON IS AN IDIOT' is written in urine. Furious, he hurries back to the oval room, and contacts his chief of security, asking him to solve the mystery. A few days later he returns and says to the President that their scientists have concluded the tests on the matter and that there is good and bad news. 'Well, give me the good news first,' Bill says.

'The good news is that it was Al Gore's urine.'

'That's the GOOD news!?' Clinton shouts, 'What's the bad news then?'

'It was Hilary's handwriting ... '

A WOMAN in distress flags down a passing traffic police car and explains that she has locked herself out of her car. The officer retrieves the old Slim Jim and proceeds to start working on the door. In the meantime, the women runs to a filling station nearby to get a pack of cigarettes. When she returns she watches the officer from the passenger-side window try to unlock the door. Instinctively she tries the door handle and discovers that it's open. 'Oops,' she announces to the officer, 'it's open!'

'I know,' answered the policeman, 'I've already done that side.'

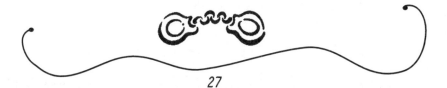

A COP was telling his partner that he and his wife of six years had a dull sex life. His partner tells him to try out a new position to add some spice into it. The cop gets home and tells his wife, 'Honey, I think we need to switch positions.' The wife smiles and says, 'Sure, you come in here and cook supper and wash the dishes and I'll lay on the couch, fart and watch TV.'

Five policemen were on a boat. The boat sank. How many policemen died?

Answer: Ten. Five during the accident, and five during the re-enactment.

THE POLICEMAN had stopped a man for obvious drunken driving, but since the guy had a clean record, he made him park the car and took him home in the patrol car. 'Are you sure this is your house?' the cop asked as they drove into a rather fashionable neighbourhood.

'Shertainly!' said the drunk, 'and if you'll just open the door f'me, I can prove it to ya.' Entering the living room, he said, 'You shee that piano? Thash mine. You shee that giant television set? Thash mine too. Now follow me.' The police officer followed the man as he shakily negotiated the stairs to the second floor.

The drunk pushed open the first door they came to. 'Thish ish my bedroom,' he announced. 'Shee the bed there? Thash mine! Shee that woman lying in the bed? Thash my wife. An' see that guy lying next to her?' 'Yeah?' the cop replied suspiciously, beginning to seriously doubt the man's story.

'Well, thash me!'

'HEY YOU! Pull over!' shouted the traffic cop. The lady complied, and the next day the judge fined her $25. She went home in great anxiety lest her husband, who always examined her cheque book, should learn of the incident. Then inspiration struck and she marked the check stub, 'One pullover, $25.'

A LOCAL man was found murdered in his home in Galveston, Texas over the weekend. Detectives at the scene found the man face down in his bathtub. The tub had been filled with milk and cornflakes, and the deceased had a banana protruding from his buttocks.
Police suspect a cereal killer.

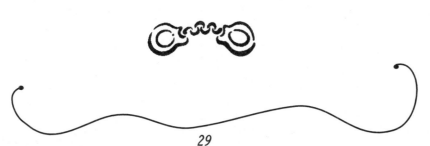

AN OLD con was talking to a new inmate in prison. 'What are ya in for, kid.'

'I tried to make a new kind of car.' He replied. 'I took the engine from a Ford, the transmission from an Oldsmobile, the tyres from a Cadillac, and the exhaust system from a Plymouth.'

'Really? What did you get?'

'Fifteen years for theft.'

A DRUNK is driving through Dublin and his car is weaving violently all over the road. One of the Gardai pulls him over. 'So,' he says to the driver, 'where have you been?'

'I've been to the pub,' slurs the drunk.

'Well,' says the cop, 'it looks like you've had quite a few.'

'I did all right,' the drunk says with a smile.

'Did you know,' says the cop, standing straight and folding his arms, 'that a few streets back, your wife fell out of your car?'

'Oh, thank heavens,' sighs the drunk. 'For a minute there, I thought I'd gone deaf.'

A YOUNG man was taking a verbal test to join the local police force. The interviewer asked, 'If you were driving a police car, alone on a lonely road at night, and were being chased by a gang of criminals driving at 60 miles an hour, what would you do?' The young man answered without a second's thought: '70!'

THERE WAS a German, an Italian and a Texas Redneck on death row. The warden gave them a choice of three ways to die:

1. was to be shot.

2. was to be hanged.

3. was to be injected with the AIDS virus.

So the German said, 'Shoot me right in the head.' (Boom, he was dead instantly.) Then the Italian said, 'Just hang me.' (Snap, he was dead.) Then the Redneck said, 'Give me some of that AIDS stuff.' They gave him the shot, and the Redneck fell down laughing. The guards looked at each other and wondered what was wrong with this guy. Then the Redneck said 'Give me another one of those shots,' so the guards did. Now he was laughing so hard, that tears rolled from his eyes and he was doubled over. Finally the warden said, 'What the hell is wrong with you?'

The Redneck replied, 'You guys are so stupid ... I'm wearing a condom!'

ONE NIGHT, a lady stumbled into the police station with a black eye. She claimed she heard a noise in her back yard and went to investigate. The next thing she knew, she was hit in the eye and knocked out cold. An officer was sent to her house to investigate, and he returned an hour and a half later with a black eye. 'Did you get hit by the same person?' his captain asked.

'Nope,' he replied. 'I stepped on the same rake.'

THE MAN was in no shape to drive, so he wisely left his car parked and walked home. As he was walking unsteadily along the pavement, he was stopped by a traffic policeman who asked him, 'What are you doing here at 2am?'

'I'm going to a lecture, officer.'

'A lecture? Who on earth is going to be giving a lecture at 2am?'

'My wife.'

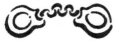

A MAN was speeding down the motorway, feeling secure in a gaggle of cars all travelling at the same speed. However, as they passed a speed trap, he got nailed with an infrared speed detector and was pulled over. The officer handed him his ticket and instructed him to appear at his local police station with all his documentation.

The driver was about to drive away when he asked, 'Officer, I know I was speeding, but I don't think it's fair – there were plenty of other cars around me who were going just as fast, so why did I get the ticket?'

'Do you fish?' the policeman asked the man.

'Yes, as a matter of fact I do.' The startled driver replied.

'Have you ever caught ALL the fish?'

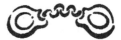

A LORRY driver was driving along a country road when a sign comes up that states: 'LOW BRIDGE AHEAD'. Before he knows it, the bridge is right in front of him and he can do nothing to stop his lorry jamming itself stuck under the bridge. Cars are backed up for miles behind him. Finally, a traffic police car arrives. The cop gets out and walks around to the lorry driver, puts his hands on his hips and says, 'Got stuck, huh?'

'No, I was delivering this bridge and ran out of derv,' the driver replies.

A MAN was driving down the road with 20 penguins in the back seat. The police stop him and say that he can't drive around with the penguins in the car and should take them to the zoo. The man agrees and drives off. The next day the same man is driving down the road with 20 penguins in the back seat again. He is stopped by the same police officer who says, 'Hey! I thought I told you to take those penguins to the zoo.'

The man replies, 'I did. Today I'm taking them to the cinema.'

AN AMERICAN police officer pulls a car over for speeding, and as he's writing the ticket out he looks at the driver carefully and says, 'Sir, I can't help but notice that your eyes are very bloodshot. Have you been drinking?'

The driver stares up at the officer and says, 'Officer, I can't help but notice that your eyes are glazed. Have you been eating donuts?'

AN AMERICAN traffic cop stops a lady and asks for her license.

'Lady, it says here that you should be wearing glasses,' he says.

The lady answers, 'Well, I do have contacts.'

'I don't care who you know! You're getting a ticket!'

FIVE-YEAR-old Little Johnny was lost, so he went up to a policeman and said, 'I've lost my dad!' The policeman said, 'What's he like?' Little Johnny replied, 'Beer and women!'

THERE WAS an inebriated driver who was pulled up by the police. When the cop opened the door, the driver fell out. 'YOU'RE DRUNK!' exclaimed the police officer. 'Thank God for that!' said the drunk, 'I thought the steering had gone.'

ONE WARM summer evening as dusk approached, a snail was sliding home from a day at the lake. Along the way, Mr. Snail had to venture into a shady part of the neighbourhood. Careful though he was, Mr. Snail was unexpectedly approached from behind by two rogue turtles. The turtles commenced to attack Mr. Snail, striking him about the head and tail with their front and rear legs. They robbed him of the valuables he carried and left him for dead. As luck would have it, a police officer on routine patrol came across the snail – still clinging on to life.

As the officer awaited medical assistance to arrive, he began his preliminary investigation into this heinous crime. 'Tell me, Mr. Snail, who did this to you?' the officer inquired.

'I don't know,' responded the snail, in obvious pain and confusion, 'it all happened so fast ... '

A MAN called 999 and spoke frantically into the phone, 'My wife is pregnant and her contractions are only two minutes apart!'

'Is this her first child?' the operator asked.

'No, you idiot!' the man shouted, 'this is her husband!'

A POLICE officer pulls over an elderly female for speeding while driving her husband to a doctors appointment. The officer approaches the vehicle and attempts to explain that he stopped her for speeding. She looks at her husband and asks, 'What did he say?' The husband replies, 'He said he stopped you for speeding.'

The officer asks the elderly female for her driver's licence and she turns and asks her husband 'What did he say?' The husband replies, 'He wants to see your driver's licence.'

The woman hands the officer her license and he sees that she is from his old home town. The officer tells the couple that he remembered the town because he had the worst sexual experience of his life there. The women looks at her husband and asks, 'What did he say?'

The husband replies, 'He says he knows you.'

A BLONDE is visiting Washington, DC. This is her first time to the city, so she wants to see the capitol building. Unfortunately, she can't find it, so she asks a police officer for directions. 'Excuse me, officer,' the blonde says, 'how do I get to the capitol building?' The officer says, 'Wait here at this bus stop for the number 54 bus. It'll take you right there.'

The blonde thanks the officer and he drives off. Three hours later the police officer comes back to the same area, and sure enough the blonde is still waiting at the same bus stop. The officer gets out of his car and says, 'Excuse me, but to get to the capitol building, I said to wait here for the number 54 bus. That was three hours ago. Why are you still waiting?'

The blonde says, 'Don't worry, officer, it won't be long now. The 45th bus just went by!'

A YUPPIE opened the door of his BMW, when a car came along suddenly and hit the door, ripping it off completely. When the police arrived at the scene, the yuppie was complaining bitterly about the damage to his precious car. 'Officer, look what they've done to my Beeeeemer!!!' he whined.

'You yuppies are so materialistic, you make me sick!!!' retorted the officer. 'You're so worried about your stupid BMW, that you didn't even notice that your left arm has been ripped off!!!'

'Oh my gaaawd ... ' replied the yuppie, finally noticing the injury, ' ... where's my Rolex?!'

Medical

THE DAY after his heart transplant a Catholic priest wakes to find his surgeon inspecting his chest. 'You're looking well, Father and the operation has been a great success. The scar will heal up nicely.'

The priest asks him, 'Can I ask you who the donor was?'

'I'm afraid that is confidential.'

'But I am a priest and am used to keeping confidences.'

'Very well,' says the surgeon, 'it was the Grand Master of the Orange Lodge of Scotland.'

'For goodness sake, how will that affect me spiritually?'

'You'll have to ask the Pope about that,' replies the surgeon.

'Who the hell is the Pope? I'm asking you!'

A DOCTOR comes home from work feeling bad about the day's activities. He lays down on the couch and ponders his actions. Like most of us, his conscience has two voices; that of his good moral side and that of his mischievous side. While staring at the ceiling, a voice in his head says, 'Don't worry about it, a lot of doctors have sex with their patients.' The man tosses and turns in reflection of his actions. Again the voice says, 'Don't worry about it, a lot of doctors have sex with their patients.'

Gradually the man begins to relax and feels a little better. Then another voice in head says, 'But you're a vet.

FOUR SURGEONS were taking a coffee break and were discussing their work. The first said, 'I think accountants are the easiest to operate on. You open them up and everything inside is numbered.'

The second said, 'I think librarians are the easiest to operate on. You open them up and everything inside is in alphabetical order.'

The third said, 'I like to operate on electricians. You open them up and everything inside is colour-coded.'

The fourth one said, 'I like to operate on lawyers. They're heartless, spineless, gutless, and their head and backside are interchangeable.'

'DOC, I can't stop singing the *Green, Green Grass of Home.*'

'That sounds like Tom Jones syndrome.'

'Is it common?'

'It's not unusual.'

A GUY goes into the doctor's 'Doc, I've got a cricket ball stuck up my arse'

'How's that?'

'Don't you start'

A GUY walks into the psychiatrist's wearing only Clingfilm for shorts.

The doctor says, 'Well, I can clearly see you're nuts.'

'Doctor, I can't pronounce my Fs, Ts and Hs.'
'Well you can't say fairer than that then.'

A WOMAN accompanied her husband to the doctor's office. After his checkup, the doctor called the wife into his office alone. He said, 'Your husband is suffering from a very severe disease, combined with horrible stress. If you don't do the following, your husband will surely die: Each morning, fix him a healthy breakfast. Be pleasant, and make sure he is in a good mood. For lunch make him a nutritious meal. For dinner prepare an especially nice meal for him. Don't burden him with chores, as he probably has had a hard day. Don't discuss your problems with him, it will only make his stress worse. And, most importantly, make love with your husband several times a week and satisfy his every whim. If you can do this for the next 10 months to a year, I think your husband will regain his health completely.'

On the way home, the husband asked his wife, 'What did the doctor say?'

'You're going to die,' she replied.

Here are some actual unedited doctor's notes on patient's charts:

1. Patient has chest pain if she lies on her left side for over a year.

2. On the 2nd day the knee was better and on the 3rd day it disappeared completely.

3. She has had no rigors or shaking chills, but her husband states she was very hot in bed last night.

4. The patient has been depressed ever since she began seeing me in 1993.

5. The patient is tearful and crying constantly. She also appears to be depressed.

6. Discharge status: Alive but without permission.

7. Healthy appearing decrepit 69-year-old male, mentally alert but forgetful.

8. The patient refused an autopsy.

9. The patient has no past history of suicides.

10. Patient has left his white blood cells at another hospital.

11. Patient's past medical history has been remarkably insignificant with only a 40 pound weight gain in the past three days.

12. Patient had waffles for breakfast and anorexia for lunch.

13. Between you and me, we ought to be able to get this lady pregnant.

14. Since she can't get pregnant with her husband, I thought you might like to work her up.

15. She is numb from her toes down.

16. While in the ER, she was examined, x-rated and sent home.

17. The skin was moist and dry.

18. Occasional, constant, infrequent headaches.

19. Patient was alert and unresponsive.

20. Rectal exam revealed a normal size thyroid.

21. She stated that she had been constipated for most of her life, until she got a divorce.

22. I saw your patient today, who is still under our car for physical therapy.

23. Patient was seen in consultation by Dr. X, who felt we should sit on the abdomen and I agree.

24. Large brown stool ambulating in the hall.

25. Patient has two teenage children, but no other abnormalities.

26. Patient appears responsive, but unable to communicate with me.

27. Bladder is under control, but cannot stop urine from seeping.

28. Heart problem is fixed. Patient died at 10.07 this morning.

29. Complains of chest pain occasionally. Otherwise just a pain.

30. Patient is always telling me about her pains and problems. This remains a significant pain to me.

31. The blood work-up showed no antibodies present. Need the rest of the blood to be sure, however.

32. If it weren't for the fact that the patient is dead, I would say he was in perfect health.

33. Testicles are missing on this woman.

A MAN comes to his doctor and tells him that his wife hasn't wanted to have sex with him for the last seven months. The doc tells the man to bring his wife in so he can talk to her. So the wife comes into the doctor's office and the doctor asks her what's wrong and why doesn't she want to have sex with her husband anymore. The wife tells him, 'For the last seven months every morning I take a cab to work. I don't have any money so the cab driver asks me, "So are you going to pay today or what?" so I take a "or what". When I get to work I'm late, so the boss asks me, "So are we going to write this down in the book or what?" So I take a "or what". Back home again I take the cab and again I don't have any money so the cab driver asks me again, "So are you going to pay this time or what?" So again I take a "or what". So you see doc when I get home I'm all tired out, and I don't want it any more.'

The doctor thinks for a second and then turns to the wife and says, 'So are we going to tell your husband or what?'

A MAN goes to his GP with a peanut stuck in his left ear.

'What can I do to get it out?' he asks pathetically.

'Pour warm chocolate in your right ear and tilt your head' replies the doctor.

'How the bloody hell will that help?'

'Easy. When the chocolate cools it should come out a treat!'

Legal

THE GREAT Jewish soldier Moshe Dyan gave a speech in which he stated that during the Six Day War he always made sure he had a battalion of lawyers ready at the front.

'That way I knew that when I shouted "Charge!" at least one battalion would know what the hell I meant.'

A LAWYER and an engineer were fishing in the Caribbean. The lawyer said, 'I'm here because my house burned down, and all I owned was destroyed by the fire. The insurance company paid for everything and I'm using some of the insurance money for this trip.'

'That's quite a coincidence,' said the engineer. 'I'm here because my house and all my belongings were destroyed by a flood, and my insurance company also paid for everything.'

The lawyer looked somewhat confused. 'How do you start a flood?' he asked.

Actual transcripts from court proceedings:

Lawyer: What gear were you in at the moment of the impact?
Witness: Gucci sweats and Reeboks.

Lawyer: What was the first thing your husband said to you when he woke that morning?
Witness: He said, 'Where am I, Cathy?'
Lawyer: And why did that upset you?
Witness: My name is Susan.

Lawyer: Did you blow your horn or anything?
Witness: After the accident?
Lawyer: Before the accident.
Witness: Sure, I played for ten years. I even went to school for it.

Lawyer: Now doctor, isn't it true that when a person dies in his sleep, he doesn't know about it until the next morning?

Lawyer: Were you present when your picture was taken?

Lawyer: Was it you or your younger brother who was killed in the war?

Lawyer: Did he kill you?

Lawyer: How far apart were the vehicles at the time of the collision?

Lawyer: You were there until the time you left, is that true?

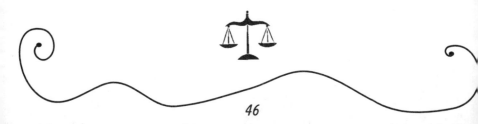

Lawyer: She had three children, right?
Witness: Yes.
Lawyer: How many were boys?
Witness: None.
Lawyer: Were there any girls?

Lawyer: How was your first marriage terminated?
Witness: By death.
Lawyer: And by whose death was it terminated?

Lawyer: Can you describe the individual?
Witness: He was about medium height and had a beard.
Lawyer: Was this a male, or a female?

Lawyer: Is your appearance here this morning pursuant to a deposition notice which I sent to your attorney?
Witness: No, this is how I dress when I go to work.

Lawyer: Doctor, how many autopsies have you performed on dead people?
Witness: All my autopsies are performed on dead people.

Lawyer: All your responses must be oral, OK? What school did you go to?
Witness: Oral.

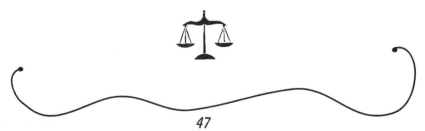

Lawyer: Do you recall the time that you examined the body?

Witness: The autopsy started around 8.30pm.

Lawyer: And Mr. Dennington was dead at the time?

Witness: No, he was sitting on the table wondering why I was doing an autopsy.

Lawyer: Doctor, before you performed the autopsy, did you check for a pulse?

Witness: No.

Lawyer: Did you check for breathing?

Witness: No.

Lawyer: So, then it is possible that the patient was alive when you began the autopsy?

Witness: No.

Lawyer: How can you be so sure, Doctor?

Witness: Because his brain was sitting on my desk in a jar.

Lawyer: But could the patient have still been alive nevertheless?

Witness: It is possible that he could have been alive and practising law somewhere.

Lawyer: What did the tissue samples taken from the victim's vagina show?

Witness: There were traces of semen.

Lawyer: Male semen?

Witness: That's the only kind I know of.

Lawyer: Did you ever sleep with him in New York?

Witness: I refuse to answer that question.

Lawyer: Did you ever sleep with him in Chicago?

Witness: I refuse to answer that question.
Lawyer: Did you ever sleep with him in Miami?
Witness: No.

Lawyer: So after the anaesthetic, when you came out of it, what did you observe with respect to your scalp?
Witness: I didn't see my scalp the whole time I was in hospital.
Lawyer: It was covered?
Witness: Yes. Bandaged.
Lawyer: Then, later on, what did you see?
Witness: I had a skin graft. My whole buttocks and leg were removed and put on top of my head.

Clerk: Please repeat after me: I swear by almighty God ...
Witness: I swear by almighty God.
Clerk: That the evidence that I give ...
Witness: That's right.
Clerk: Repeat it.
Witness: Repeat it.
Clerk: No! Repeat what I said.
Witness: What you said when?
Clerk: That the evidence that I give ...
Witness: That the evidence that I give.
Clerk: Shall be the truth and ...
Witness: It will, and nothing but the truth!
Clerk: Please, just repeat after me: Shall be the truth and ...
Witness: I'm not a scholar, you know.
Clerk: We can appreciate that. Just repeat after me: Shall be the truth and ...

Witness: Shall be the truth and.

Clerk: Say: Nothing ...

Witness: Okay. (Witness remains silent.)

Clerk: No! Don't say nothing. Say: Nothing but the truth ...

Witness: Yes.

Clerk: Can't you say: Nothing but the truth ... ?

Witness: Yes.

Clerk: Well? Do so.

Witness: You're confusing me.

Clerk: Just say: Nothing but the truth ...

Witness: Is that all?

Clerk: Yes.

Witness: Okay. I understand.

Clerk: Then say it.

Witness: What?

Clerk: Nothing but the truth ...

Witness: But I do! That's just it.

Clerk: You must say: Nothing but the truth ...

Witness: I WILL say nothing but the truth!

Clerk: Please, just repeat these four words: Nothing ... but ... the ... truth.

Witness: What? You mean, like, now?

Clerk: Yes! Now. Please. Just say those four words.

Witness: Nothing. But. The. Truth.

Clerk: Thank you.

Witness: I'm just not a scholar.

A PIPE burst in a lawyer's house, so he called a plumber. The plumber arrived, unpacked his tools, did mysterious plumber-type things for a while, and handed the lawyer a bill for £600. The lawyer exclaimed, 'This is ridiculous! I don't even make that much as a lawyer!' The plumber quietly replied, 'Neither did I when I was a lawyer.'

Sex and Marriage

A COUPLE married for 40 years were revisiting the same places they went to on their honeymoon. Driving through the secluded countryside, they passed a farm with a tall deer fence running along the road. The woman said, 'Sweetheart, let's do the same thing we did here 40 years ago.' The guy stopped the car. His wife backed against the fence and they made love like never before. Back in the car, the guy says, 'Darling, you never moved like that 40 years ago – or any time since, that I can remember!'

His wife replied, 'That fence wasn't electrified 40 years ago!'

A RATHER confident man walks into a bar and takes a seat next to a very attractive woman. He gives her a quick glance, then casually looks at his watch for a moment. The woman notices this and asks, 'Is your date running late?' 'No', he replies, 'I just bought this state-of-the-art watch and I was just testing it.' The intrigued woman says, 'A state-of-the-art watch? What's so special about it?' 'It uses alpha waves to telepathically talk to me,' he explains.

'What's it telling you now?' she says.

'Well, it says you're not wearing any panties.'

The woman giggles and replies, 'Well it must be broken then because I am wearing panties!'

The man leans towards her and confides, 'Damn thing must be an hour fast!'

A WORRIED father telephoned his family doctor and said that he was afraid that his teenage son had come down with VD. 'He says he hasn't had sex with anyone but the maid, so it has to be her.'

'Don't worry so much,' advised the doctor. 'These things happen.'

'I know, doctor,' said the father, 'but I have to admit that I've also been sleeping with the maid. I seem to have the same symptoms.'

'That's unfortunate.'

'Not only that, I think I've passed it to my wife.'

'Oh God,' said the doctor, 'That means we all have it.'

A WOMAN was trying to board a bus, but her skirt was too tight and she couldn't step up. She reached behind her and lowered her zipper a bit and tried again. The skirt was still too tight. She reached behind her and lowered the zipper some more. She still couldn't get on the bus and lowered the zipper a third time. All of a sudden, she felt two hands on her bottom, and she was pushed up onto the bus. She spun around, with anger in her eyes and said very indignantly, 'Sir, I do not know you well enough for you to behave in such a manner.'

The man smiled coyly and said, 'Lady, I don't know you well enough either for you to unzip my fly three times.'

A GUY goes into a bar with his pet octopus and says 'I bet £50 that no one here has a musical instrument that this octopus can't play.' The people in the bar look around and someone fetches out an old guitar. The octopus has a look, picks it up, tunes up the strings and starts playing the guitar. The octopus' owner pockets the money.

Next guy comes up with a trumpet, the octopus takes the horn, loosens up the keys, licks its lips and starts playing a jazz solo. The guy hands over another £50 to the octopus' owner. The bar owner has been watching all this and disappears out back, coming back a few moments later with a set of bagpipes under his arm. He puts them on the bar and says to the guy and his octopus, 'Now, if your octopus can play that I'll give you £100.'

The octopus takes a look at the bagpipes, lifts it up, turns it over, has another look from another angle. Puzzled, the octopus's owner comes up and says 'What are you messing around for? Hurry up and play the damn thing!' The octopus says, 'Play it? If I can work out how to get its pyjamas off I'm going to have sex with it!'

A YOUNG, trendy married couple was invited to a swanky masked Halloween Party. Before going, the wife got a terrible headache and told her husband to go to the party alone. He, being a devoted husband, protested, but she argued and said she was going to take some aspirin and go to bed, and there was no need for his good time being spoiled by not going. So he took his costume and away he went.

The wife, after sleeping soundly for one hour, awakened without pain and as it was still early, she decided to go the party. Her husband did not know what her costume was, so she thought she would have some fun by watching her husband to see how he acted when she was not with him. She joined the party and soon spotted her husband cavorting around on the dance floor, dancing with every babe he could, and copping a little feel here and a little kiss there.

His wife sidled up to him and being a rather seductive babe herself, he left his partner high and dry and devoted a little time to this new bit of stuff that had just arrived.

She let him go as far as he wished; naturally, as he was her husband. Finally, he whispered a little proposal to her and she agreed, so off they went to one of the cars and had sex. Just before unmasking at midnight, she slipped away, went home, put the costume away and got into bed, wondering what kind of explanation he would make for his behaviour.

She was sitting up reading when he came in and asked what kind of a time he had had. He said, 'Oh, the same old thing. You know I never have a good time when you're not there.' Then she asked, 'Did you dance much?' He replied, 'I'll tell you, I never even danced one dance. When I got there, I met Pete, Bill and some other guys, so we went into the games room and played snooker all evening. But you're not going to believe what happened to the guy I loaned my costume to ...'

A husband is at home watching a football game when his wife interrupts. 'Honey, could you fix the light in the hallway? It's been flickering for weeks now.' He looks at her and says angrily 'Fix the light? Now? Does it look like I have a Scottish Power logo printed on my forehead? I don't think so.'

'Well then, could you fix the fridge door? It won't close right.' To which he replies, 'Fix the fridge door? Does it look like I have SMEG written on my forehead? I don't think so.'

'Fine' she says. 'Then could you at least fix the steps to the front door? They're about to break.'

'I'm not a damn joiner and I don't want to fix the steps,' he says. 'Does it look like I have Ace Construction written on my forehead? I don't think so. I've had enough of you ... I'm off to the pub!'

So he goes to the pub and drinks for a couple of hours. He starts to feel guilty about how he treated his wife, and decides to go home and help out. As he walks into the house, he notices that the steps are already fixed. As he enters the house, he sees that the hall light is working, and as he goes to get a beer, he notices that the fridge door is fixed. 'Honey, how did all this get fixed?'

She replied 'Well, when you left, I sat outside and cried. Just then a nice young man asked me what was wrong, and I told him. He offered to do all the repairs, and in return all I had to do was either have sex with him or bake him a cake.'

The husband says, 'So, what kind of cake did you bake him?'

'Helllloooooo ... do you see Delia Smith written on my forehead? I don't think so!'

There once was a man who was so proud of the fact that he had six kids that he insisted on calling his wife 'mother of six'. His wife hated this name and asked him repeatedly not to call her that, but he was a stubborn man and was very proud that he had six kids. One evening they were at a dinner party for his company and it was getting close to the time that they should be leaving. The husband yelled from across the room over to his wife: 'Mother of six, are you ready to go?'

Furious with him, she trumpeted across the room: 'In a minute, father of four!'

Getting married is very much like going to a restaurant with friends. You order what you want, then when you see what the other person has, you wish you had ordered that.

At a cocktail party, one woman said to another, 'Aren't you wearing your wedding ring on the wrong finger?'

The other replied, 'Yes, I am, I married the wrong man.'

After a quarrel, a husband said to his wife, 'You know, I was a fool when I married you.' She replied, 'Yes, dear, but I was in love and didn't notice.'

A lady inserted an ad in the classifieds: Husband wanted. Next day she received a hundred letters. They all said the same thing: You can have mine.

When a woman steals your husband, there is no better revenge than to let her keep him.

Eighty per cent of married men cheat in America. The rest cheat in Europe.

Man is incomplete until he is married. Then he is finished.

A little boy asked his father, 'Daddy, how much does it cost to get married?' And the father replied, 'I don't know son, I'm still paying.'

Young Son: Is it true, Dad, I heard that in some parts of Africa a man doesn't know his wife until he marries her?

Dad: That happens in every country, son.

Then there was a man who said, 'I never knew what real happiness was until I got married; and then it was too late.'

A woman was telling her friend, 'It is I who made my husband a millionaire.'

'And what was he before you married him?' asked the friend. The woman replied, 'A billionaire.'

'The trouble with being the best man at a wedding is that you never get to prove it.'

Marriage is the triumph of imagination over intelligence. Second marriage is the triumph of hope over experience.

If you want your spouse to listen and pay strict attention to every word you say, talk in your sleep.

Just think, if it weren't for marriage, men would go through life thinking they had no faults at all.

You know the honeymoon is pretty much over when you start to go out with the boys on Wednesday nights
    … And so does she.

During a heated spat over finances the husband said, 'Well, if you'd learn to cook and were willing to clean this place, we could fire the maid.'

The wife, fuming, shot back, 'Oh yeah??? Well, if you'd learn how to make love, we could fire the chauffeur and the gardener.'

One of the greatest things about marriage is that as both husband and father, you can say anything you want to around the house. Of course, no one pays the least bit of attention.

According to the latest surveys, when making love, most married men fantasise that their wives aren't fantasising.

My girlfriend told me I should be more affectionate. So I got two girlfriends.

How do most men define marriage? A very expensive way to get your laundry done free.

The most effective way to remember your wife's birthday is to forget it once.

Words to live by: Do not argue with a spouse who is packing your parachute.

First guy (proudly): 'My wife's an angel!'
Second guy: 'You're lucky, mine's still alive.'

WOMEN WILL never be equal to men until they can walk down the street with a bald head and a beer gut, and still think they are beautiful.

A FREE Church of Scotland minister is visiting Glasgow with his wife for a shopping trip. Before dinner in their hotel the minister agrees to meet his wife at the bar as she isn't quite ready yet. At the bar the minister sits beside an attractive girl and they strike up a conversation.

'And tell me, my dear, what sort of work do you do?'

'I'm a call girl,' replies the girl.

The minister looks thrilled and exclaims, 'Well, I'll be ... I'm from Tiree myself!'

America

Here are some examples of ACTUAL announcements made on domestic US airline flights:

1.   There may be 50 ways to leave your lover, but there are only four ways out of this airplane.

2.   Folks, we have reached our cruising altitude now, so I am going to switch the seat belt sign off. Feel free to move about as you wish, but please stay inside the plane till we land ... it's a bit cold outside, and if you walk on the wings it affects the flight pattern.

3.   Thank you for flying Delta Business Express. We hope you enjoyed giving us the business as much as we enjoyed taking you for a ride.

4.   As the plane landed and was coming to a stop at Washington National, a lone voice comes over the loudspeaker: 'Whoa, big fella ... WHOA!'

5.   After a particularly rough landing during thunderstorms in Memphis, a flight attendant on a Northwest flight announced: 'Please take care when opening the overhead compartments because, after a landing like that, sure as hell everything has shifted.'

6. From a Southwest Airlines employee: 'Welcome aboard Southwest Flight XXX to YYY. To operate your seatbelt, insert the metal tab into the buckle, and pull tight. It works just like every other seatbelt and if you don't know how to operate one, you probably shouldn't be out in public unsupervised. In the event of a sudden loss of cabin pressure, oxygen masks will descend from the ceiling. Stop screaming, grab the mask, and pull it over your face. If you have a small child travelling with you, secure your mask before assisting with theirs. If you are travelling with two small children, decide now which one you love more.'

7. Weather at our destination is 50 degrees with some broken clouds, but they'll try to have them fixed before we arrive. Thank you, and remember, nobody loves you or your money, more than Southwest Airlines.

8. Your seat cushions can be used for flotation and in the event of an emergency water landing, please take them with our compliments.

9. As you exit the plane, please make sure to gather all of your belongings. Anything left behind will be distributed evenly among the flight attendants. Please do not leave children or spouses.

10. Last one off the plane must clean it.

11. From the pilot during his welcome message: 'We are pleased to have some of the best flight attendants in the industry. Unfortunately none of them are on this flight.'

12. An American Airlines flight into Amarillo, Texas, on a particularly windy and bumpy day: During the final approach, the captain was really having to fight it. After an extremely hard landing, the flight attendant came on the PA and announced, 'Ladies and Gentlemen, welcome to Amarillo. Please remain in your seats with

your seatbelts fastened while the captain taxis what's left of our airplane to the gate!'

13. Another flight attendant's comment on a less than perfect landing: 'We ask you to please remain seated as Captain Kangaroo bounces us to the terminal.'

14. An airline pilot wrote that on a particular flight he had hammered his ship into the runway really hard. The airline had a policy which required the first officer to stand at the door while the passengers exited, smile, and give them a 'Thanks for flying XYZ airline.' He said that in light of his bad landing, he had a hard time looking the passengers in the eye, thinking that someone would have a smart comment. Finally, everyone got off except for this little old lady walking with a cane. She said, 'Sonny, mind if I ask you a question?'
'Why no, Ma'am,' said the pilot, 'what is it?'
The little old lady said, 'Did we land or were we shot down?'

15. After a real crusher of a landing in Phoenix, the flight attendant came on the tannoy with, 'Ladies and Gentlemen, please remain in the aircraft until we come to a screeching halt up against the gate. And, once the tire smoke has cleared and the warning bells are silenced, we'll open the door and you can pick your way through the wreckage to the terminal.'

16. Part of a flight attendant's arrival announcement: 'We'd like to thank you folks for flying with us today. And, the next time you get the insane urge to go blasting through the skies in a pressurised metal tube, we hope you'll think of us here at US Airways.'

The last four US presidents are caught in a tornado, and off they spin to OZ. After threatening trials and tribulations, they finally make it to the Emerald City and come before the Great Wizard.

'WHAT BRINGS YOU BEFORE THE GREAT WIZARD? WHAT DO YOU WANT?' he booms.

Jimmy Carter steps forward timidly:

'I had a terrible time with Iran, so I've come for some courage.'

'No problem,' says the Wizard,

'WHO IS NEXT?'

Ronald Reagan steps forward, 'Well ... well ... er ... well, I need a brain.'

'Done,' says the Wizard.

'WHO COMES NEXT BEFORE THE GREAT WIZARD?'

Up steps George Bush sadly, 'I'm told by the American people that I need a heart.'

'I've heard it's true,' says the Wizard. 'Consider it done.'

Then there is a great silence.

Bill Clinton is just standing there, looking around, not saying a word.

Irritated, the Wizard finally asks, 'WELL, WHAT BRINGS YOU TO THE EMERALD CITY?'

'Is Dorothy around?'

CORPORATE AMERICA

After a two-year long study, The National Science Foundation announced the following results on Corporate America's recreational preferences:

1. The sport of choice for male unemployed or incarcerated people is BASKETBALL

2. The sport of choice for male maintenance-level employees is BOWLING

3. The sport of choice for male front-line workers is FOOTBALL

4. The sport of choice for male supervisors is BASEBALL

5. The sport of choice for male middle management is TENNIS

6. The sport of choice for male corporate officers is GOLF.

Conclusion:
The higher you are in the corporate structure, the smaller your balls are.

A farmer walked into an attorney's office wanting to file for a divorce. The attorney asked, 'May I help you?' The farmer said, 'Yea, I want to get one of those dayvorces.'

The attorney said, 'Well do you have any grounds?' The farmer said, 'Yea, I got about 140 acres.' The attorney said, 'No, you don't understand, do you have a case?' The farmer said, 'No, I don't have a Case, but I have a John Deere.'

The attorney said, 'No you don't understand, I mean do you have a grudge?' The farmer said, 'Yea, I got a grudge, that's where I park my John Deere.' The attorney said, 'No sir, I mean do you have a suit?' The farmer said, 'Yes sir, I got a suit. I wear it to church on Sundays.'

The exasperated attorney said, 'Well sir, does your wife beat you up or anything?' The farmer said, 'No sir, we both get up about 4.30.'

Finally, the attorney says, 'Okay, let me put it this way. 'WHY DO YOU WANT A DIVORCE?'

The farmer says, 'Well, I can never have a meaningful conversation with her.'

A MAN and his wife were driving through country on his way from New York to California. Looking at his fuel gauge, he decided to stop at the next gasoline station and fill up. About 15 minutes later, he spots a Mobil station and pulls over to the high octane pump.

'What can I do for ya'll?' asks the attendant. 'Fill her up with high test,' replies the driver.

While the attendant is filling up the tank, he's looking the car up and down.

'What kinda car is this?' he asks. 'I never seen one like it before.'

'Well,' responds the driver, his chest swelling up with pride, 'this, my boy is a 2000 Cadillac Seville.'

'What all's it got in it?' asks the attendant.

'Well,' says the driver, 'it has everything. It's loaded with power steering, power seats, power sunroof, digital climate control, ABS, power mirrors, AM/FM radio with a 10 deck CD player in the trunk with 100 watts per channel, eight speaker stereo, rack and pinion steering, disk brakes all around, leather interior, digital instrument package, and best of all, a 300 horsepower Northstar V8 engine which only needs a service every 100,000 miles!'

'Wow,' says the attendant, 'that's really something!'

'How much do I owe you for the gasoline?' asks the driver.

'That'll be $65,' says the attendant.

The driver pulls out his money clip and peels off a three $20 bills and a $5. He goes into his other pocket and pulls out a handful of change. Mixed up with the change are a few golf tees.

'What are those little wooden things?' asks the attendant.

'That's what I put my balls on when I'm driving,' says the driver.

'Wow,' says the attendant, '… those Cadillac people think of everything!'

That's Life

A MOTORIST was unknowingly caught in an automated speed trap and he later received in the mail a ticket for £40 and a photo of his car. Instead of payment, he sent the police department a photograph of a £40 cheque. Several days later, he received a letter from the police that contained another picture ... of a pair of handcuffs.

POLICE IN Radnor, Pennsylvania, interrogated a suspect by placing a metal colander on his head and connecting it with wires to a photocopier. The message 'He's lying' was placed in the copier, and police pressed the copy button each time they thought the suspect wasn't telling the truth.

Believing the 'lie detector' was working, the suspect confessed.

LITTLE JOHNNY'S kindergarten class was on a field trip to their local police station where they saw pictures, tacked to a bulletin board, of the 10 'most wanted men'. One of the youngsters pointed to a picture and asked if it really was the photo of a wanted person. 'Yes,' said the policeman. 'The detectives want him very badly.' Little Johnny asked, 'So, why didn't you keep him when you took his picture?'

A YOUNG woman was doing some business at Marshall University and parked in an area clearly marked 'No Parking'. After her meeting, she returned to her car to find a campus security guard writing her a ticket. 'Why are you giving me a ticket?' she asked. 'You're not allowed to park here,' the guard said. 'See that sign? It says "Fine for Parking Here".'

'Well,' said the lady, 'I thought it meant it was fine to park there.'

The guard began to laugh. The more he thought about it, the harder he laughed. He tore up the ticket and waved the woman on her way.

FIVE BELGIANS in an Audi Quattro arrive at the French border. The French customs agent stops them and says: 'It's illegal to put five people in a Quattro.'

'No, Quattro is just the name of the automobile. Look at the papers: this car is designed to carry five persons.'

'You can't pull that one on me,' replies the French customs agent. 'Quattro means four!'

'You are so stupid! Call your supervisor over!'

'He can't come. He's busy with the two guys in the Fiat Uno'

THE STRONG young man at the construction site was bragging that he could outdo anyone in a feat of strength. He made a special case of making fun of one of the older workmen. After several minutes, the older worker had enough. 'Why don't you put your money where your mouth is?' he said. 'I will bet a week's wages that I can haul something in a wheelbarrow over to that outbuilding that you won't be able to wheel back.'

'You're on, old man,' the braggart replied. 'Let's see what you got.'

The old man reached out and grabbed the wheelbarrow by the handles. Then, nodding to the young man, he said, 'All right. Get in.'

THREE GUYS kick the bucket on Christmas Eve and ascend to heaven where they are met by St. Peter. 'In honour of the season,' St. Peter says to them, 'you must each possess something that symbolises Christmas.'

The first man fumbles through his pockets and pulls out two lighters. He holds them up proudly and flicks them on.

'What do they symbolise?' St. Peter asks him.

'They're candles!'

'Ah! You may pass through the pearly gates!'

The second man fumbles through his pockets and pulls out a couple sets of keys. He holds them up proudly and shakes them.

'What do they symbolise?' St. Peter asks.

'They're bells!'

'Ah! You may pass through the pearly gates!'

The third man fumbles desperately through his pockets, finally pulling out a skimpy pair of silky woman's panties. He holds them up proudly.

'And what do those symbolise?' St. Peter asks.

'They're Carol's!'

A BUSINESSMAN from Aberdeen went on a business trip to Louisiana. Upon arrival, he immediately plugged his laptop into the hotel room port and sent a short e-mail back home to his wife, Jennifer Johnson, at her address, JennJohn@world.net.

Unfortunately, in his haste, he mistyped a letter and the e-mail ended up going to JeanJohn@world.net, a Jean Johnson in Selkirk, the wife of a minister who had just passed away and had been buried that day. The preacher's wife took one look at the e-mail and promptly fainted.

It read, 'Arrived safely, but it sure is hot down here!'

SEEMS AN elderly gentleman had serious hearing problems for a number of years. He went to the doctor who was able to have him fitted for a hearing aid that allowed the gentleman to hear 100 per cent. The elderly gentleman went back in a month to the doctor who said, 'Your hearing is perfect. Your family must be really pleased that you can hear again.' To which the gentleman said, 'Oh, I haven't told my family yet. I just sit around and listen to the conversations. I've changed my will three times!'

THIS BLOKE'S in bed with his missus when there's a rat-a-tat-tat on the door. He rolls over and looks at his clock, and it's half three in the morning. Sod that for a game of soldiers, he thinks, and rolls over. Then, a louder knock follows. 'Aren't you going to answer that, Dave?' says his wife so he drags himself out of bed, and goes downstairs. He opens the door and this bloke is stood outside. 'Eh mate,' says the stranger, 'can you give us a push?'

'No, now bugger off, it's half three. I was in bed.'

Dave shuts the door and goes back up to bed and tells his wife what happened. She then says, 'Dave, you are a twat. Remember that night we broke down in the pouring rain on the way to pick the kids up from the babysitter and you had to knock on that man's house to get us started again? What would have happened if he'd told us to bugger off?' So Dave gets out of bed again, gets dressed, and goes downstairs. He opens the door, and not being able to see the stranger anywhere he shouts, 'Eh mate, do you still want a push?' and he hears a voice cry out, 'Yeah, please mate.' So, still being unable to see the stranger he shouts: 'Where are you?' and the stranger replies, 'I'm over here on the swings.'

THREE OLDER gals were chatting about the problems of ageing gracefully. One said, 'Sometimes I catch myself with a jar of mayonnaise in my hand, in front of the refrigerator, and can't remember whether I need to put it away, or start making a sandwich.'

The second lady chimed in, 'Oh yes, Ethel, sometimes I find myself standing on the stairs and can't remember whether I was on my way up or on my way down.'

The third one responded, 'Well, I'm glad I don't have that problem; knock on wood,' as she rapped her knuckles on the table. Suddenly she said, 'Oh, darn! Someone at the door, I'll get it!'

SO THERE'S this blonde out for a walk. She comes to a river and sees another blonde on the opposite bank. 'Yoo-hoo!' she shouts, 'How can

I get to the other side?' The second blonde looks up the river then down the river then shouts back:

'You are on the other side!'

A GUY comes home completely drunk one night. He lurches through the door and is met by his scowling wife, who is most definitely not happy.

'Where the hell have you been all night?' she demands.

'At this fantastic new bar,' he says. 'The Golden Saloon. Everything there is golden. It's got huge golden doors, a golden floor, the works. Hell, even the urinal's gold!'

The wife still doesn't believe his story, and the next day checks the phone book, finding a place across town called the Golden Saloon. She calls up the place to check her husband's story.

'Is this the Golden Saloon?' she asks when the bartender answers the phone.

'Yes it is,' bartender answers.

'Do you have huge golden doors?'

'Sure do.'

'Do you have golden floors?'

'Most certainly do.'

'What about golden urinals?'

There's a long pause, then the woman hears the bartender yelling, 'Hey, Duke, I think I got a lead on the guy that pissed in your saxophone last night!'

An 85-year-old couple, after being happily married for almost 60 years, die together in a car crash. They have been in good health the

last ten years, mainly due to mum's interest in health food and proper diet. When they reach the Pearly Gates, St. Peter takes them to their luxury mansion, which is decked out with a beautiful kitchen, master bedroom suite and a fancy in-house jacuzzi. The old man asks St. Peter how much all this was going to cost.

'It's free,' St. Peter replies, 'this is Heaven.'

Next, they go out the back yard to survey the championship-style golf course that the home overlooks. They would have golfing privileges every day. In addition, the course changed to a new one daily, representing the greatest golf courses on Earth.

The old man asks, 'So, what are the green fees?'

St. Peter replied, 'This is Heaven, you play for free!'

Next, they go to the clubhouse and see the lavish buffet lunch with the best cuisine of the World laid out. 'How much to eat?' asks the old man.

'Don't you understand yet? This is Heaven, it is free!!' St. Peter replies with some exasperation.

'Well, where are the low fat and low cholesterol tables?' the old man asks timidly. In a forceful voice, St. Peter says, 'That's the best part, you can eat as much as like of whatever you like and you never get fat and you never get sick. This is Heaven!'

With that, the old man goes into a fit of anger, throwing down his halo, screaming wildly and taking the Lord's name in vain. St. Peter and his wife both try to calm him down, asking what is wrong. The old man glares at his wife and says, 'This is all your fault! If it weren't for your blasted bran muffins, I could have been here years ago!'

AN AMISH boy and his father were visiting a mall. They were amazed by almost everything they saw, especially two shiny walls that could move apart, and back together again.

The boy asked his father, 'What is this father?' The father (having never seen an elevator) responded, 'Son, I have never seen anything like this in my life, I don't know what it is.'

While the boy and his father were watching wide-eyed, an old lady, limping slightly, and with a cane, slowly walks up to the moving walls, and presses a button. The walls opened, and the lady walks between them, into a small room. The walls closed.

The boy and his father watched as small circles of lights with numbers above the wall light up. They continued to watch the circles light up, in reverse direction now.

The walls opened up again, and a beautiful young blonde stepped out.

The father turned to his son, 'GO GET YOUR MOTHER!!!'

AN ELDERLY man lay dying in his bed. In death's agony, he suddenly smelled the aroma of his favourite chocolate chip cookies wafting up the stairs. He gathered his remaining strength, and lifted himself from the bed. Leaning against the wall, he slowly made his way out of the bedroom, and forced himself down the stairs. Gripping the railing with both hands, he crawled downstairs. With laboured breath, he leaned against the door-frame gazing into the kitchen. Were it not for death's agony, he would have thought himself already in heaven: there, spread out upon waxed paper on the kitchen table were literally hundreds of his favourite chocolate chip cookies. Was it heaven? Or was it one final act of heroic love from his devoted wife, seeing to it that he left this world a happy man?

Mustering one great final effort, he threw himself toward the table, landing on his knees in a crumpled posture. His parched lips parted: the wondrous taste of the cookie was already in his mouth, seemingly bringing him back to life. His aged and withered hand trembled on its way to a cookie at the edge of the table, when it was suddenly smacked with a spatula by his wife.

'Bugger off,' she said, 'these are for your funeral.'

A GIRL asks her boyfriend to come over one Friday night and have dinner with her parents. Since this is such a big event, the girl announces to her boyfriend that after dinner, she would like to go out and have sex for the first time. Well, the boy is ecstatic, but he has never had sex before, so he takes a trip to the pharmacist to get some condoms. The pharmacist helps the boy for about an hour. He tells the boy everything there is to know about condoms and sex. At the register, the pharmacist asks the boy how many condoms he'd like to buy, a three-pack, ten-pack or the family pack. The boy insists on the family pack because he thinks he will be rather busy, this being his first time.

That night, the boy shows up at the girl's parents' house and meets his girlfriend at the door. 'Oh I'm so excited for you to meet my parents, come on in!' The boy goes inside and is taken to the dinner table where the girl's parents are seated. The boy quickly offers to say grace and bows his head. A minute passes, and the boy is still deep in prayer, with his head down. Ten minutes pass, and still no movement from the boy. Finally, he quickly offers to say grace again and bows his head.

A minute passes, and the boy is still deep in prayer, with his head down. Ten minutes pass, and still no movement from the boy. Finally, after twenty minutes with his head down, the girlfriend finally leans over and whispers to the boyfriend, 'I had no idea you were this religious'. The boy turns, and whispers back, 'I had no idea your father was a pharmacist.'

A RUSSIAN couple were walking down the street in Moscow one

night, when the man felt a drop hit his nose. 'I think it's raining,' he said to his wife. 'No, that felt more like snow to me,' she replied. 'No, I'm sure it was just rain,' he said. Well, as these things go, they were about to have a major argument about whether it was raining or snowing, when they saw a Communist Party official walking towards them. 'Let's not fight about it,' the man said, 'Let's ask Comrade Rudolph whether it's officially raining or snowing.'

As the official approached, the man said, 'Tell us, Comrade Rudolph, is it officially raining or snowing?'

'It's raining, of course,' he replied, and walked on.

But the woman insisted: 'I know that felt like snow!' To which the man quietly replied: 'Rudolph the Red knows rain, dear.'

A BLOKE has locked his car keys inside his vehicle. He stands by the side of his car looking completely fed up when a chap walks up and asks him what the problem is.

'I've locked my car keys in my car and can't get in,' says the first individual. 'No problem mate,' says the second chap. 'Stand to one side and I'll get you in.' The first chap does as he's asked and stands to one side. The second chap moves in front of the door handle, turns around, and rubs his backside against the door lock. Almost instantly the car door unlocks. 'Strewth!' says the first fella, 'How did you manage that?' 'Easy,' says the second bloke, 'I'm wearing my Khaki trousers.'

A SAILOR comes round and finds himself on a beach. He opens his eyes and sees that the sea is purple, the sand is purple, the sky is purple, the grass is purple. He looks at his hands and they are purple.

It is then he realises that he has been marooned.

A LITTLE old lady walked into the head branch of the Chase Manhattan Bank holding a large paper bag in her hand. She told the young man at the window that she wished to take the $3 million she had in the bag and open an account with the bank. She said that first, though, she wished to meet the president of Chase Manhattan Bank due to the amount of money involved.

The teller seemed to think that was a reasonable request and after opening the paper bag and seeing the bundles of $1000 bills he telephoned the bank president's secretary to obtain an appointment. The lady was escorted upstairs and ushered into the president's office. Introductions were made and she stated that she liked to get to know the people she did business with on a personal level. The bank president then asked her where she came into such a large sum of money.

'Was it an inheritance?' he asked.

'No.' she replied.

'Was it from playing the stock market?' he inquired.

'No.' she answered.

He was quiet for a minute, trying to think of where this little old lady could possibly have come into $3 million.

'I bet.' she stated.

'You bet?' repeated the bank president. 'As in horses?'

'No,' she replied, 'I bet people.'

Seeing his confusion, she explained that she just bets different things with people. All of a sudden she said, 'I'll bet you $25,000 that by 10 o'clock tomorrow morning your testicles will be square.' The bank president figured she must be off her rocker and decided to take her up on the bet. He didn't see how he could lose. For the rest of the day, the bank president was very careful. He decided to stay home that evening and take no chances, there was $25,000 at stake. When he got up in the morning and took his shower, he checked to make sure everything was okay. There was no difference, he looked the same as he always had.

He went to work and waited for the little old lady to come in at 10am, humming as he went. He knew this would be a good day: how often do you get handed $25,000 for doing nothing? At 10am sharp the little old lady was shown into his office. With her was a younger man. When he enquired as to the man's purpose for being there, she informed him that he was her lawyer and she always took him along when there was this much money involved.

'Well,' she asked, 'what about our bet?'

'I don't know how to tell you this,' he replied, 'but I'm the same as I've always been, only $25,000 richer. The lady seemed to accept this, but requested that she be able to see for herself. The bank president thought this was reasonable and dropped his trousers. She instructed him to bend over and then grabbed a hold of him. Sure enough, everything was fine. The bank president then looked up and saw her lawyer standing across the room banging his head against the wall.

'What's wrong with him?' he enquired.

'Oh him,.' she replied. 'I bet him $100,000 that by 10.30 this morning I'd have the President of Chase Manhattan Bank by the balls.'

A SCOTSMAN emigrates to the United States and shortly after, attends his first ever baseball game. After a hit, he hears the fans roaring, 'Run ... run!' The following batter connects heavily with the ball and the Scotsman stands up and roars with the crowd in his thick accent, 'Run, yah bloody baahstard, run!' A third batter smacks a hard line drive and again the Scotsman – obviously pleased with his knowledge of the game – screams, 'Run, yah bloody baahstard, run why don't ya?' The next batter takes a pitch on a three and two count and the umpire calls, 'Take your base.' Foolishly, the Scotsman stands, yelling, 'Run, ya baahstard, run!' All the surrounding fans giggle quietly so he sits down confused. A friendly fan, sensing the Scot's embarrassment, whispers, 'He doesn't have to run, he's got four balls.' The Scotsman stands up in disbelief and shouts, 'Ahh, for God's sake man! Walk with pride! Walk with pride!'

HARRY HAD a bit of a drinking problem. Every night, after dinner, he took off for the local watering hole. He spent the whole evening there, and arrived home, well inebriated, around midnight each night. He always had trouble getting his key into the keyhole, and getting the door opened. His wife, waiting up for him, would go to the door and let him in. Then she would proceed to yell and scream at him, for his constant nights out, and coming home in a drunken state. But Harry continued his nightly routine.

One day, the wife was talking to a friend about her husband's behaviour, and was particularly distraught by it all. The friend listened to her, and then said, 'Why don't you treat him a little differently when he comes home? Instead of berating him, why don't you give him some loving words, and welcome him home with a kiss? Then he might change his ways.' The wife thought it was worth trying. That night, Harry took off again after dinner. And, about midnight, he arrived home, in his usual condition. His wife heard him at the door, quickly went to it, opened the door, and let Harry in. This time, instead of berating him, as she had always done, she took his arm, and led him into the living room. She sat him down in an easy chair, put his feet up on the footstool and took his shoes off. Then she went behind him, and started to cuddle him a little. After a while, she said to him, 'It's pretty late. I think we had better go upstairs to bed now, don't you?'

At that, Harry replied, in his inebriated state, 'I guess we might as well. I'll get in trouble when I get home anyway!'

A MAN takes his Great Dane to the vet. 'My dog's cross-eyed, is there anything you can do for him?' 'Well,' says the vet, 'let's have a look at him.' So he picks the dog up and examines his eyes, then checks his teeth. Finally, he says 'I'm going to have to put him down.'

'What? Because he's cross-eyed?'

'No, because he's bloody heavy.'

THIS BLOKE is sitting reading his *Evening Herald* newspaper when the wife sneaks up behind him and whacks him on the head with a frying pan. 'What was that for?' he asks.' That was for the piece of paper in your trouser pocket with the name Mary-Ellen written on it,' she replies. 'Don't be daft,' he explains '... two weeks ago when I went to the races, Mary-Ellen was the name of one of the horses I bet on.'

She seems satisfied and at this apology and goes off to do work around the house.

Three days later he's again sitting in his chair reading when she nails him with an even bigger frying pan, knocking him out cold. When he comes around he says, 'What the heck was that for?'

'Your horse phoned!'

After Dinner and one liners

Did you hear why the LA Police had to leave the Dodgers' game early?
To beat the crowd.

ONE DAY an old lady was driving along the motorway steering with her feet and knitting as she went. She was swerving all over the road when a traffic police car drew up alongside her. The policeman shouts over, 'Pull over!' The lady replies, 'No it's socks!'

What did the Bra say to the hat?
'You go on ahead, I'll give these two a lift.'

What's the difference between a goldfish and a goat?
One mucks about in fountains.

How do crazy people go through the forest?
They take the psycho path.

How do you get holy water?
Boil the hell out of it.

What did the fish say when he hit a concrete wall?
'Dam'.

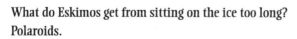

What do Eskimos get from sitting on the ice too long?
Polaroids.

What is the difference between snowmen and snowwomen?
Snowballs.

Why do only 30 per cent of women get into heaven?
If it were more, it would be hell.

Q: How can you tell if you're at a bulimic bachelor party?
A: The cake jumps out of the girl.

Q: If your wife keeps coming out of the kitchen to nag at you, what
have you done wrong?
A: Made her chain too long.

Q: Do you know why women fake orgasm?
A: Because men fake foreplay.

Q: A woman of 35 thinks of having children. What does a man of 35
think of?
A: Dating children.

Q: What's the difference between a G-Spot and a golf ball?
A: A guy will actually search for a golf ball.

Q: What did the elephant say to the naked man?
A: It's cute but can you pick up peanuts with it?

Q: What did the slug say to the snail?
A: 'Want to buy a *Big Issue*?'

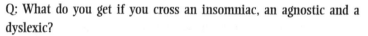

Q: What do you get if you cross an insomniac, an agnostic and a dyslexic?
A: Someone who stays up all night wondering if there is a dog.

A couple of cows were standing in a field at Borve in Berneray. One asked the other, 'Are you not scared of catching BSE?'
The other replied 'No, I'm pretty safe because I'm a hen!'

A man from Point sat in the Coffee Pot in Stornoway for eight hours, just staring at a carton of orange juice. When asked what he was doing he said 'Look, it says "concentrate"!'

Q: What do you call a fly with no wings?
A: A walk.

A horse walked into the doctors' surgery at Griminish in Benbecula and the receptionist said, 'Excuse me, but why the long face?'

What's the difference between a man and a catfish?
One is a bottom-feeding scum-sucker and the other is a fish.

Husband: Want a quickie?
Wife: As opposed to what?

Why do men want to marry virgins?
They can't stand criticism.

I went to the county fair. They had one of those 'Believe it or not' shows.

They had a man born with a penis and a brain.

What do you have when you have two little balls in your hand?
A man's undivided attention.

What are two reasons why men don't mind their own business?
1. No mind.
2. No business.

A neutron walks into a bar and asks how much a pint is?
The barman replies, 'For you, no charge.'

Q: Where does Saddam Hussein keep his CDs?
A: In Iraq

Q: Why do golfers have two pairs of trousers?
A: In case they get a hole in one.

And Finally ...

MINISTRY OF DEFENCE
WHITEHALL LONDON SW1A 2HB

Telephone 0171-21 82111/2/3

SECRETARY OF STATE

Mr Ali Abbasi,   25 5 98
BBC Radio Sotland
Queen Margaret Drive
Glasgow G12

Dear Ali,

I was most concerned that you not had an acknowledgement of your letter of congratulations. I hope that a year later you will accept this as a heartfelt thanks.

After four years dealing with Scottish politics and press it was a refreshing change to have only to deal with President Sadaam Hussein, Radovan Karadic, President Suharto, the PIRA, war criminals, pirates and drug-runners. However I remember, with fond recollection some - well, a few - aspects of my job as Shadow Scottish Secretary.

One of them, it has to be said, was constantly meeting the McIntyre / Abbasi duo – both legends in their time. In particular I recall the fact that one always wanted stories to retell and the other told stories you never could re-tell.

I will continue to rely on your splendid and totally accurate road reports. Who needs the Global Positioning Satellite system when Ali Abasi is there on the airwaves?

Yours ever,

George

Recycled Paper